THOMAS

The COURAGEOUS Series

BOOK 2

GOD'S COURAGEOUS MISSIONARY

VOMBOOKS
The Voice of the Martyrs

Thomas: God's Courageous Missionary

VOM Books
1815 SE Bison Rd.
Bartlesville, OK 74006

ISBN 978-0-88264-208-6

Written by The Voice of the Martyrs with Cheryl Odden

Illustrated by G. R. Erlan

Printed in China

CPC-201908p001d2

For our Christian family members in India
who suffer for their faith in Jesus Christ

A Note to Parents and Educators

Of all the apostles martyred for their Christian witness, Thomas is perhaps the most talked about. More has been written about his apostleship to India in songs, poems, and stories than about his discipleship in the Gospels. Christians in India still celebrate his arrival with the gospel and his martyrdom in their country.

Born in Galilee, Thomas was among the original twelve disciples called by Jesus. His career remains a mystery, but some assume he was a fisherman (John 21). Of the references to Thomas in the Gospels, his words are recorded only in the Book of John.

When the disciples object to Jesus going to Judea where Lazarus has died, Thomas' first recorded words are, "Let us also go, that we may die with Him." The disciples knew the Jews in Judea threatened to stone Jesus, yet a willing Thomas courageously rallies the troops. They go to Judea, and Jesus raises Lazarus from the dead to glorify God. The Jews and Jesus' disciples witness a resurrection, solidifying belief that Jesus is God's Son. Jesus then shares one of His eight "I am" statements: "I am the resurrection and the life." But in the end, it takes a dramatic demonstration to get Thomas to believe.

During the Last Supper, Jesus again calls the disciples to believe in Him, telling them He will prepare a place for them. Thomas unabashedly asks, "Lord, we do not know where you are going. How can we know the way?" Perhaps not grasping the spiritual kingdom of Jesus, Thomas thought He was going to some glorious physical city where He would reign. Jesus responds with another "I am" statement: "I am the way, the truth, and the life. No one comes to the Father except through Me." Once again, Jesus tells them that if they have seen Jesus, they have seen the Father.

Thomas' final exchanges are found in the closing chapters of John, after Christ's death and resurrection. Thomas stares in disbelief when several disciples tell him about Jesus' after-death appearances. "Unless I see in his hands the mark of the nails, and place my finger into the mark of the nails, and place my hand into his side, I will never believe," asserts Thomas. Because of these words, he has been called "Doubting Thomas."

But days later, Jesus appears again to the disciples and Thomas. Looking at Thomas, Jesus challenges the skeptic: "Put your finger here, and see my hands; and put out your hand, and place it in my side. Do not disbelieve, but believe."Immediately, Thomas cries out, "My Lord and my God!"

After Jesus ascended to heaven, history tells us the apostles divided the known world among themselves to evangelize. According to one account, for Thomas the lot fell to India, along with Ethiopia and Parthia (in modern-day Iran). At that time, "Ethiopia" included Africa (as we know it today) and parts of Persia. But it was in India that Thomas was martyred. Several traditions recount Thomas' mission in India.

In the Indian tradition, passed down orally through the centuries, Thomas arrived around AD 50 or 52 on India's Malabar Coast, which is a major spice exporting port even today. He is credited with founding seven churches. Thousands turned to Christ through his ministry, with one source claiming thousands of conversions just from among the Hindu priests, rulers, and merchants, in addition to two kings and seven village chiefs. This story claims that Thomas preached east and west on the subcontinent, and one tradition suggests he even went to China.

According to Indian tradition, Thomas was martyred around AD 70 by Brahmin priests performing a ritual. Thomas challenged them and won, but then they killed him.

Today in India, there is a group of Christians who trace their origins to the apostle Thomas. Called "St. Thomas Christians," they have used songs and poetry to maintain this tradition through the centuries.

Thomas' grave is on a hill called St. Thomas Mount at Mylapore, where he is believed to have been killed. Over the centuries, artifacts have been discovered to provide evidence of his adventures on the mostly Hindu subcontinent. Liturgies in the Near East's ancient churches credit Thomas with being India's first apostle, pointing those in India to the same Jesus who told him, "I am the way, the truth, and the life."

As your children read about this doubter turned faith-filled missionary, may they be inspired by Thomas' trust in God. And may the story encourage and lead them on their own faith adventure to share the gospel with their friends.

"**L**et's go back to Judea and see Lazarus," said Jesus. Lazarus was very sick, and the time was right for a miracle, to show that Jesus was the Son of God.

"But Master," said one, "the Jews in Judea want to kill you. Are You going there again?"

One disciple was not afraid. His name was Thomas. He stood up and said, "Let's all go, and die with Him!"

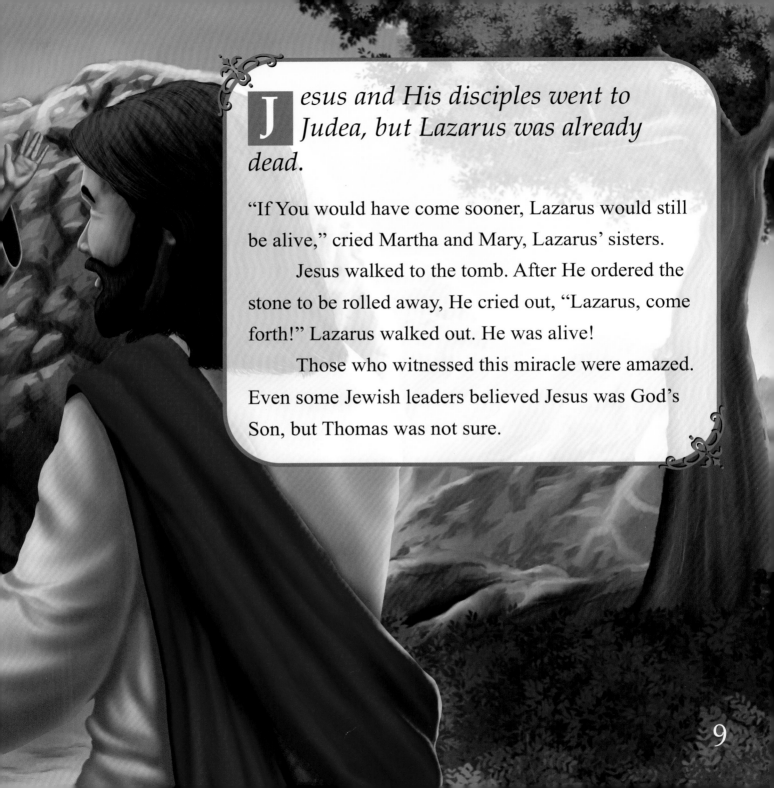

Jesus and His disciples went to Judea, but Lazarus was already dead.

"If You would have come sooner, Lazarus would still be alive," cried Martha and Mary, Lazarus' sisters.

Jesus walked to the tomb. After He ordered the stone to be rolled away, He cried out, "Lazarus, come forth!" Lazarus walked out. He was alive!

Those who witnessed this miracle were amazed. Even some Jewish leaders believed Jesus was God's Son, but Thomas was not sure.

One evening as Jesus ate dinner with Thomas and the other disciples, He told them that He was going to die on the cross.

"Don't worry," said Jesus, comforting His disciples who were saddened by the news. "You trust God, don't you? Now you need to trust Me. You know where I am going and how to get there."

"Lord, we do not know where You are going," said Thomas, confused. "How can we know the way?"

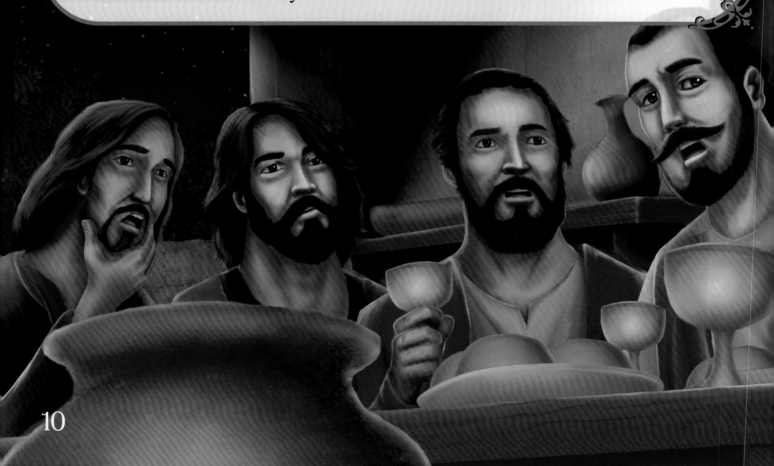

Jesus looked into Thomas' bewildered face and said, "I am the way, the truth, and the life. No one comes to the Father except through Me."

11

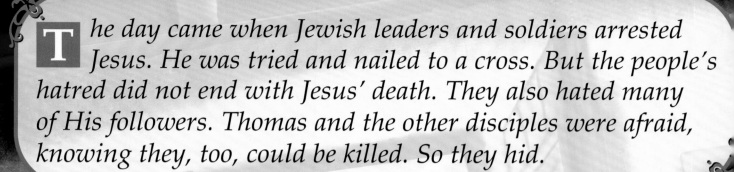

The day came when Jewish leaders and soldiers arrested Jesus. He was tried and nailed to a cross. But the people's hatred did not end with Jesus' death. They also hated many of His followers. Thomas and the other disciples were afraid, knowing they, too, could be killed. So they hid.

Bang! The disciples burst through the door. "Thomas!" they shouted, unable to contain their excitement. "We saw Jesus. He's alive!"

Thomas shook his head in disbelief. *Impossible!* thought Thomas as his eyes narrowed into a scowl. *He's gone forever.*

"I don't believe you," he snapped.

"But Thomas, we saw Him!" they repeated.

"I'll believe it only if I see in His hands the holes from the nails and put my fingers into them."

Eight days later the disciples were again hiding in a locked room. Jewish leaders still roamed the streets hunting down anyone claiming to follow Jesus. Suddenly, Jesus appeared to them!

"Put your finger here in My hands," Jesus said, looking right at Thomas. "Don't be a doubter. Believe!"

"My Lord and my God!" cried Thomas. Seeing Jesus' scars was the proof he needed.

"You believe because you have seen Me," said Jesus. "Blessed are those who have not seen and yet believe."

Later, Thomas would give his life for those who had not seen Jesus and yet believed.

Thomas and the other ten disciples gathered on a mountain in Galilee.

Jesus appeared to them and gave them His final instructions before He returned to heaven.

"Go and make followers of Me in all nations," He told them.

The day finally came when Thomas walked through the gates of Jerusalem, carrying with him only what he needed.

Like the other apostles, he started his journey to spread the gospel to the ends of the earth. His travels would take him to a strange and exotic place.

21

Before Thomas arrived in India, he traveled through Persia (called Iran today), where many had not yet heard about Jesus.

Thomas preached about Jesus Christ and His free gift of eternal life. Many placed their trust in the Savior.

23

Soon Thomas knew his time in Persia was done, so he boarded a ship and left for India.

PERSIA

PERSIAN GULF

INDIA

25

26

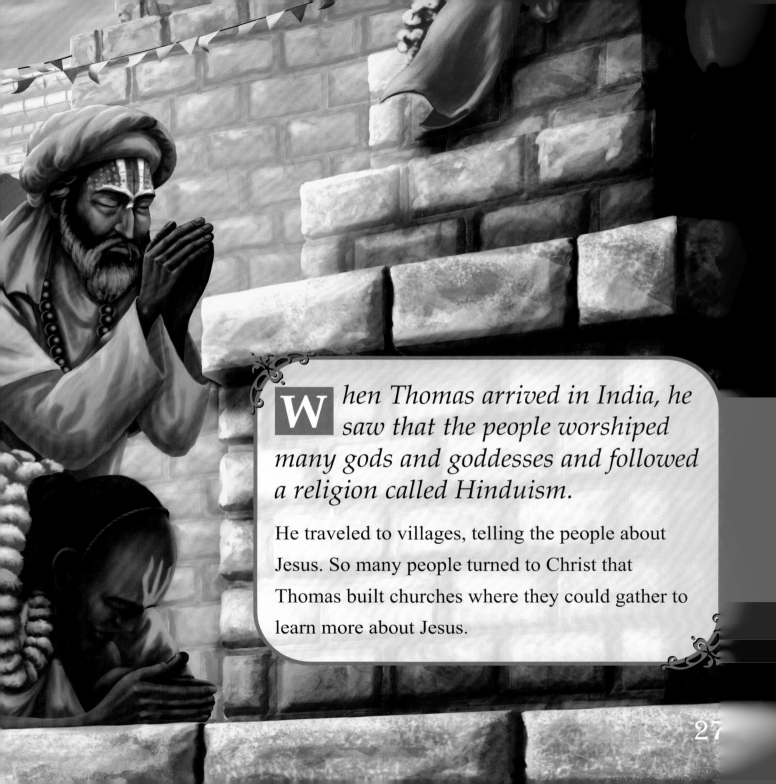

When Thomas arrived in India, he saw that the people worshiped many gods and goddesses and followed a religion called Hinduism.

He traveled to villages, telling the people about Jesus. So many people turned to Christ that Thomas built churches where they could gather to learn more about Jesus.

27

When the people turned to Christ, they left their false gods and goddesses and burned their Hindu temples.

Some Hindus were furious with Thomas for turning people away from their religion, which began in their country long before Jesus was born. Soon Thomas would face their anger, and it would cost him his life.

29

S ome say that one day, Thomas met a group of Hindu priests whose actions puzzled him. They were tossing water into the air while chanting their prayers.

"Why are you doing that?" asked Thomas.

"The water is our sacrifice to the gods," they replied.

"Then why aren't your gods accepting it?" asked Thomas, who watched as the water droplets kept returning to the ground.

Surely the priests thought this strange-looking man was crazy.

"Who can make the water hang in the air?" mocked the priests.

"I can," claimed Thomas.

"Then prove it!" they said.

T homas' face brightened as he saw his chance to tell them about Jesus.

"I will prove it to you," he replied. "But only if you promise to believe in God's Son and be baptized if I succeed."

The priests agreed to the deal. How could they lose? They would prove Thomas wrong.

Thomas walked up to the basin, cupped the cool water in his hands, and tossed it up into the air.

The priests looked up into the blue sky, waiting for the drops to fall to the ground. But they didn't. Some say the water drops hung in the air and sparkled like diamonds!

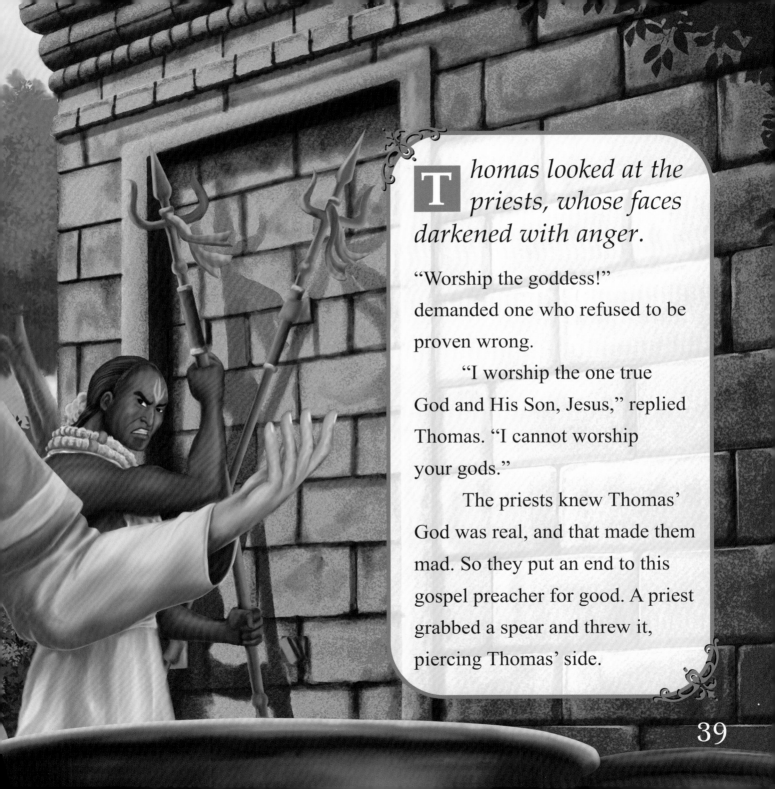

Thomas looked at the priests, whose faces darkened with anger.

"Worship the goddess!" demanded one who refused to be proven wrong.

"I worship the one true God and His Son, Jesus," replied Thomas. "I cannot worship your gods."

The priests knew Thomas' God was real, and that made them mad. So they put an end to this gospel preacher for good. A priest grabbed a spear and threw it, piercing Thomas' side.

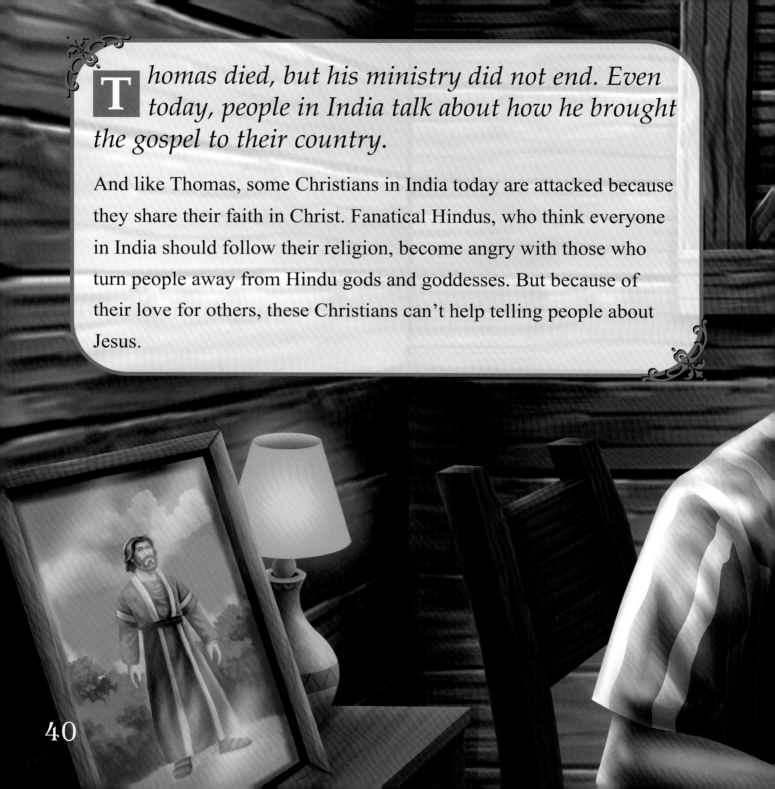

Thomas died, but his ministry did not end. Even today, people in India talk about how he brought the gospel to their country.

And like Thomas, some Christians in India today are attacked because they share their faith in Christ. Fanatical Hindus, who think everyone in India should follow their religion, become angry with those who turn people away from Hindu gods and goddesses. But because of their love for others, these Christians can't help telling people about Jesus.

When you tell a friend about Jesus, remember: God promises to give you that same faith and courage that He gave to Thomas in India. All you have to do is ask, and the next step is yours!

For Reflection

"And I was with you in weakness and in fear and much trembling, and my speech and my message were not in plausible words of wisdom, but in demonstration of the Spirit and of power, so that your faith might not rest in the wisdom of men but in the power of God."
(1 Corinthians 2:3–5)

Before Jesus died on the cross, did Thomas believe that Jesus was the Son of God? How about after Jesus rose from the dead?

What does it mean to have a strong faith in Jesus? Why was it important for Thomas to have a strong faith in Jesus before he went to Persia and then India?

Do you think Thomas felt scared when he challenged the priests in India?

When you tell a friend about Jesus, do you feel scared?

According to these verses, what does God promise to do when we tell others about Jesus even when we're scared?

Prayer

Dear Jesus,
Thank You for the example of Thomas, who once doubted You but later became strong in faith and took the gospel to India. When I share about You with my friends, please give me the power that You promise, even if I feel scared.
I pray for Christians in India who are opposed because they tell others about You.
I pray that You will also strengthen their faith.

Amen.

Bibliography

Foxe, John and The Voice of the Martyrs. *Foxe: Voices of the Martyrs* (Washington, D.C.: Salem Books, 2019).

Holman QuickSource Bible Atlas (Nashville, TN: Holman Bible Publishers, 2005).

Huc, Évariste Régis. *Christianity in China, Tartary, and Thibet, Volume I* (London: Longman, Brown, Green, Longmans, & Roberts, 1857).

Moffett, Samuel Hugh. *A History of Christianity in Asia, Volume I: Beginnings to 1500* (Maryknoll, NY: Orbis Books, 1998).

Neill, Stephen. *A History of Christianity in India: The Beginnings to AD 1707* (New York: Cambridge University Press, 1984).

Van Braght, Thieleman J. *Martyrs Mirror* (Scottdale, PA: Herald Press, 1994).

About The Voice of the Martyrs

The Voice of the Martyrs (VOM) is a nonprofit, interdenominational Christian missions organization dedicated to serving our persecuted Christian family worldwide through practical and spiritual assistance and leading other members of the body of Christ into fellowship with them. VOM was founded in 1967 by Pastor Richard Wurmbrand, who was imprisoned fourteen years in Communist Romania for his faith in Christ, and his wife, Sabina, who was imprisoned for three years. In 1965, Richard and his family were ransomed out of Romania and established a global network of missions dedicated to assisting persecuted Christians.

Be inspired by the courageous faith of our persecuted brothers and sisters in Christ and learn ways to serve them by subscribing to VOM's free monthly magazine. Visit us at persecution.com or call 1-800-747-0085. Explore VOM's five purposes and statement of faith at persecution.com/about.